CONTENTS

Dedication	ii
About the Author	iii
1. The Supermom Myth	1
2. Time Management for the Time-Starved	13
3. Parenting as a Process	29
4. Money Matters	42
5. Knowing Your Team	47
6. Self-Care	66
CONCLUSION	79

DEDICATION

To my mom, Julie-Julz-Nanny-Bananny. You could make any job, even cleaning the stockyards, fun. You had the biggest heart and gave the best hugs. Thank you for teaching me how to work hard and make best chocolate chip cookies. Your love, and lessons will always be my guide.

ABOUT THE AUTHOR

Raised in the wide-open spaces of Montana, Tanya is the proud mom of five amazing girls. When she's not wrangling her lively crew, she's been busy building a remarkable career supporting the US Nuclear Navy. A graduate of Boise State University, she holds a bachelor's degree in Electrical and Computer Engineering and has spent over 15 years working for the Department of Defense. From Montana's mountains to Guam's tropical shores, she's managed to balance a high-tempo career with the everyday challenges of motherhood, all with a sense of humor and a love for the beautiful chaos that comes with raising five daughters.

CHAPTER 1

The Supermom Myth (And Why You Should Ignore It)

1.1 Lowering the Bar (It's More Fun Down Here)

If you've ever been a first-time manager, you know the feeling: you walk into the role thinking you've got to be perfect. You have high expectations for yourself, convinced that you'll be the boss who always knows the right answer, keeps everyone happy, and runs things smoothly. Then reality hits. Suddenly, you're learning as you go, figuring out not just how to manage people but also how to manage yourself.

Being a mom—especially for the first time—is a lot like that. You think you've got to be Supermom, raising perfect children while maintaining a spotless house and a Pinterest-worthy lifestyle. But here's the thing: no one actually knows what they're doing at the start, not managers, not moms. You're figuring out how to parent and lead at the same time, and that's no easy task.

And yes, you'll feel judged. You'll hear comments from everyone—other parents, friends, and even strangers in the grocery store—about what you should be doing. Just like in a new leadership role, there's always someone with an opinion on how you should handle things. The real challenge is tuning out that noise and finding the leadership style—or in this case, the mom style—that works for you and your kids.

Much like managing a team, motherhood isn't about achieving some perfect standard. It's about learning what works, making mistakes, and adjusting as you go. So lower that bar. You don't have to be perfect—you just have to find your own rhythm, the one that fits your life and your family. And guess what? You'll get better at it, just like you did in your first management role. The key is to let go of the pressure to be flawless and focus on being the best version of yourself. After all, the kids aren't looking for perfection; they're looking for a mom who's present, authentic, and willing to laugh when things don't go according to plan.

In the end, being a good leader—and a good mom—means finding the balance between doing your best and giving yourself grace when things inevitably fall apart. And trust me, they will. But that's part of the journey. So, lower that bar, take a deep breath, and remember: it's all about progress, not perfection.

Another similarity between being a new manager and a mom is that you often feel like you're under a microscope. At work, you have employees watching your every move, maybe waiting to see if you know what you're doing. In motherhood, you feel that same pressure, except this time it's from society, friends, or even social media—where everyone seems to have it all together, and you're wondering why your kid refuses to wear pants today.

In both cases, you'll feel like you're failing sometimes. Maybe a project didn't go as planned at work, or your kids had ice cream for dinner because you couldn't deal with one more meltdown. The trick is realizing that these moments don't define you as a manager or a mother. They're part of the process, part of learning how to lead and nurture in your own way.

Just like in management, the trick to motherhood is figuring out what works for you. You don't need to follow someone else's rulebook or adhere to impossible standards. Sure, you'll read advice books, get unsolicited opinions, and hear about all the things "good" moms supposedly do, but at the end of the day, you'll develop your own style. Maybe your management style is more laid-back, or maybe you're a hands-on type of leader. As a mom, maybe you're the type to make crafts with the kids, or maybe your strength is showing them how to problem-solve on their own. The point is, the sooner you let go of unrealistic expectations, the sooner you'll find what works for your family.

Here's the fun part: lowering the bar doesn't mean you're not trying hard or that you don't care. It means you're smart enough to know that perfection is unattainable, and that sanity, joy, and balance are worth much more. Some days, you'll crush it at work and make it to soccer practice with snacks ready. Other days, it'll feel like you're failing at everything—and that's okay. It's all part of figuring out your groove.

So just like in management, cut yourself some slack. There's no one "right" way to be a boss or a mom. You're doing the best you can with what you've got—and that's enough. As you get more comfortable with the chaos (both in the office and at home), you'll find that lowering the bar is actually the secret to feeling more accomplished. Because when the goal is "do your best," you'll always hit the mark.

Lowering the bar gives you room to breathe, laugh, and enjoy the ride, knowing that you're growing into this role at your own pace. That's the real victory.

1.2. The Miracle of Setting Realistic Expectations (And Why It's Hard)

If you're a career-driven woman, the idea of anything less than perfection can feel… unacceptable. You're used to deadlines, deliverables, and excelling in your field. You've built a reputation for being competent, reliable, and probably a little bit of a perfectionist. So, when motherhood comes along and throws you into a world where nothing is predictable and mistakes happen daily, it's hard to let go of that desire for perfection.

Here's the thing, though: would you ever expect someone new to a job to be perfect? Of course not. You'd give them room to learn, time to adjust, and you'd celebrate their progress, not their perfection. Motherhood is no different. It's a job you've never done before—one with constantly changing expectations and no clear metrics for success. You're going to make mistakes, but just like in your career, that's how you learn.

When setting expectations for yourself as a mom, remember that the days are long, but the years are short. In the moment, it's easy to get caught up in the idea that everything has to go perfectly—that you have to be everywhere, do everything, and never drop the ball. But zoom out a bit. It's not about having everything run smoothly every single day. It's about showing up and doing your best, day after day, even when things are messy.

Perfection isn't the goal here—consistency is. It's about being present for your kids, even when you feel like you're only giving 50%. They don't need a flawless, magazine-cover mom; they need you. Most kids aren't going to remember whether dinner was homemade or if your house was spotless. What they'll remember is that you were there—tired but trying, frustrated but still loving.

In your career, you probably excel by planning, anticipating, and staying two steps ahead. But as a mom, flexibility is key. You can't plan for every tantrum or spilled cereal, and you definitely can't predict when your toddler will decide that pants are no longer an acceptable life choice. Just like you wouldn't fire an employee for missing a deadline in their first week, you can't expect yourself to master this whole motherhood thing overnight—or even in a few years.

It's hard to lower your standards when you've spent your career raising the bar, but the reality is that your best on any given day is enough. Some days, your best will look like nailing that work presentation, getting dinner on the table, and making it to story time with your kids. Other days, your best will look like sending a few emails and keeping everyone fed (even if it's just cereal for dinner). And that's okay.

So give yourself permission to set realistic expectations. Some days will feel like wins, and some days won't. But remember that motherhood, like any career, is a marathon, not a sprint. It's about showing up, trying your best, and understanding that your "best" might look different from day to day. You don't have to be perfect—you just have to keep going, knowing that your love and effort matter far more than perfection ever could.

1.3. Embrace and Romanticize Your Life: The Power of Gratitude

Life as a working mom, juggling deadlines, school runs, and finding matching socks in the laundry abyss, can feel overwhelming. But in the chaos, there's one thing that can shift your perspective faster than a child asking "what's for dinner" for the 12th time in an hour: gratitude. Romanticizing your life doesn't mean pretending everything is perfect. It's about noticing the beauty in the small, everyday moments. It's watching your kids giggle uncontrollably and appreciating the way they light up when they see you after work. It's feeling the warmth of your morning coffee and taking a moment to breathe before the day begins. By reframing the ordinary, you begin to see your life for what it really is: full of moments worth celebrating.

There's something almost magical about taking a moment to acknowledge the things that are going right, even when everything feels like it's falling apart. It doesn't mean you ignore the challenges or pretend life is perfect (because we all know it's not), but by focusing on the good, you give yourself a mental reset. You start to see the silver linings you might have otherwise missed.

Science backs this up. Studies show that practicing gratitude can have a profound impact on your overall well-being. When you focus on what you're grateful for, it triggers biological responses in your brain. Gratitude stimulates the production of dopamine and serotonin—the "feel-good" chemicals that promote happiness and reduce stress. Over time, this rewires your brain to focus more on the positive aspects of your life, helping you to find joy even in the most chaotic days.

Gratitude also reduces stress levels, improves sleep, and strengthens relationships. By acknowledging and appreciating what's going well, you shift your mindset from one of scarcity (always feeling like there's not enough time, not enough progress) to one of abundance. You begin to notice that, despite the challenges, there's always something to be thankful for.

Growing up, my mom had this tactic whenever one of us had a bad attitude: the Glad Game. It's exactly what it sounds like—a game where we had to go around the room and say what we were glad for. My sisters and I would roll our eyes at first, thinking it was silly. But by the time we all said something—anything—we were glad about, something strange would happen. The mood in the room would lighten, and the bad attitudes would melt away. We'd laugh, realizing how much we actually had to be happy about. Suddenly, the fact that we were mad about not getting dessert or being told to clean our room seemed less important. Life seemed pretty great, after all.

As an adult, I've come to realize my mom was onto something. When things feel out of control, pausing to acknowledge the little (or big) things we're grateful for can be a game-changer. It doesn't have to be grand. Sometimes it's as simple as being glad your kids didn't fight on the way to school or that the coffee machine still works. Whatever it is, there's always something worth appreciating.

The Gratitude Challenge

To help you embrace your life and cultivate a more positive mindset, here's a challenge: for the next 30 days, keep a gratitude journal. Each day, write down one thing you're thankful for or the happiest moment of your day. It doesn't have to be monumental—it could be something as small as a quiet moment with your kids or an unexpectedly smooth commute. The important thing is to notice those little moments and embrace them. Over time, you might find that even on the toughest days, there's always a bright spot worth acknowledging.

Why a journal? Writing down what you're grateful for reinforces those positive thoughts. It's like giving your brain a little nudge to pay attention to the good stuff. And on days when you're feeling overwhelmed, you can flip back through your entries and be reminded of all the things that bring joy to your life, even on the hard days.

Here are a few prompts to get you started:

- What was one moment today that made you smile?

- Who in your life are you most grateful for today, and why?

- What small thing did you do today that made you feel proud?

By the end of the 30 days, you'll likely notice a shift. You'll start to find beauty in the everyday moments, and you'll feel more connected to the life you're living, even if it's not the picture-perfect version you imagined.

Remember, it's not about being perfect; it's about being present. It's about showing up, embracing the chaos, and choosing to focus on the little things that make life beautiful. Romanticize the simple moments, and watch how your mindset shifts. After all, this is your story—you get to decide how to see it.

CHAPTER 2

Time Management for the Time-Starved

2.1. Planning Like a Pro (With a Side of "No, Thanks")

Let's talk about planning, shall we? As a mom, your calendar probably looks like a chaotic blend of school events, sports practices, work meetings, birthday parties, and maybe—just maybe—a sliver of time for yourself. It's tempting to look at that rare white space and think, "I should fill this with something." But here's the truth: just because your calendar has some breathing room doesn't mean you need to fill it! In fact, sometimes the best plan is to not make any plans at all.

One of the hardest lessons in motherhood—and life—is learning to protect your energy and say "no" when necessary. You don't have to RSVP to every event or sign up for every committee just because there's time available. If something makes you feel anxious, drained, or out of place, it's okay to politely decline. Your mental health and well-being are worth far more than an afternoon at an event where you feel like a fish out of water. And guess what? People will survive without you there!

The same goes for your kids. It's easy to fall into the trap of thinking they need to participate in everything—soccer, dance, karate, pottery, underwater basket weaving (is that still a thing?). But before you sign up for the next sport or club, take a step back. Ask yourself: do they really want to do this, or is it just something that sounds good on paper? And more importantly, do you have the time and energy to make it happen?

Every new activity comes with hidden costs—both time and money. Saturday soccer practice sounds fun until you realize you'll be spending every weekend ferrying them to games in neighboring towns, all while keeping up with the gear, snacks, and fees. Be selective. It's okay to have your kids in one or two activities that they genuinely enjoy rather than trying to keep up with everyone else who's booked solid with activities seven days a week.

Here's the golden rule: you don't have to be busy to be a good mom. Protect your "you" time. Whether it's a quiet coffee in the morning before the chaos begins or a weekend afternoon where you don't have to be anywhere, these pockets of time are sacred. They allow you to recharge so that when you do show up—for work, your kids, or that occasional event you do want to attend—you're doing it with full energy and a positive mindset, not feeling like you're scraping the bottom of the energy barrel.

So, embrace the joy of saying "no." Say "no" to the things that drain you and don't serve your priorities. Say "no" to the pressure to fill every hour. And say "no" to that little voice in your head that tells you a good mom is a busy mom. You're allowed to guard your time, protect your peace, and keep your calendar as light as you need it to be.

The value is in quality, not quantity—both in how you spend your time and what your kids are doing. You know what's not fun? Running from a ballet recital to soccer practice to a birthday party, all in the span of four hours, only to arrive at each one looking like you just competed in a triathlon (because let's face it, you basically did). When you're stretched thin, no one is getting the best version of you—not your kids, not your friends, and certainly not the poor barista who had to make your third coffee of the day while you sprinted through the drive-thru.

Instead, focus on quality. It's not about attending every event or cramming in as many activities as humanly possible. It's about showing up—fully present—for the things that truly matter to you and your kids. Believe it or not, your kids won't remember the packed schedule where they were in a different activity every day of the week. They'll remember the moments where you were fully there—cheering them on at the one sport they actually love or spending an afternoon together, just hanging out.

Let's face it: there's no award for the mom who fills up the most calendar space. No one is handing out trophies for who can juggle the most commitments, and even if they were, do you really want one of those? What would you even do with a "Most Overbooked Mom" award? Stick it on your already overcrowded shelf, probably right next to the participation trophies from the sports your kids didn't even like?

It's way more valuable to have a few things on your plate that you can truly enjoy and commit to. Because when you're not running around like a madwoman, you actually get to enjoy these moments. You can cheer at soccer games without being distracted by the next appointment. You can chat with other moms at the bake sale without mentally running through the fifty things you still have to do. And maybe, just maybe, you'll even get to sit on the couch and enjoy a show (you know, one episode of something that doesn't involve animated talking animals).

Quality time is where the real magic happens. You don't need to fill your schedule to the brim to make memories or be a great mom. In fact, scaling back might just give you the chance to savor the moments you do have. Fewer commitments mean less stress, more connection, and—let's be real—a better chance of getting through the week without losing your mind.

So, give yourself permission to prioritize quality over quantity. Let your calendar breathe a little. Pick the things that bring you joy and the ones that make your kids light up. And feel free to say "no" to the rest. Because at the end of the day, your worth as a mom isn't measured by how much you can cram into 24 hours. It's measured by the love, laughter, and presence you bring to the time you have. There's a lot more of that to go around when you're not in constant sprint mode!

2.2. The Myth of Multitasking (And Why You Should Stop Trying)

For busy moms, multitasking can feel like a superpower. After all, when you're juggling work, kids, and housework, it seems like the only way to get everything done. But here's the hard truth: multitasking is a myth. We've all been sold the idea that we can do multiple things at once effectively, but in reality, when we think we're multitasking, we're just bouncing between tasks—and doing all of them poorly.

Studies have shown that our brains aren't wired to focus on more than one complex task at a time. Each time you switch from answering an email to supervising homework, then back to an email or onto dinner prep, your brain has to stop and reorient itself. This constant switching not only slows you down but also increases stress and the likelihood of making mistakes. So, instead of doing everything at once, it's time to rethink how we approach our endless to-do lists.

One way to tackle this is by adopting a more intentional approach, like the one found in Stephen Covey's 7 Habits of Highly Effective People. Covey teaches the power of prioritization through a simple but effective time-management strategy: categorizing tasks by urgency and importance. By understanding what's truly critical, you can focus on what needs to be done right now, rather than spreading yourself thin across tasks that don't require immediate attention.

Covey's model breaks tasks down into four quadrants:

1. Urgent and Important: These are your top priorities—deadlines for work, a doctor's appointment for your child, or anything that absolutely must happen now. Focus most of your energy here.

2. Important but Not Urgent: These are tasks that matter in the long run but don't have immediate deadlines, like long-term career goals, personal development, or spending quality time with family. It's easy to put these off, but they are crucial for personal and professional growth.

3. Urgent but Not Important: These tasks demand attention but don't contribute to your bigger goals, like answering non-essential emails or dealing with distractions. These are the time-wasters, and Covey suggests minimizing them as much as possible.

4. Neither Urgent nor Important: These tasks should be avoided if possible. Think mindlessly scrolling social media or other activities that neither serve your long-term goals nor require immediate attention.

The key to effective task management is to spend as much time as possible in the Important but Not Urgent quadrant—where planning, goal-setting, and relationship-building live—while still tackling those urgent priorities when needed. This approach will help you avoid getting trapped in reactive mode, where you feel like you're constantly putting out fires without making meaningful progress.

So, instead of trying to get everything done at once, focus on getting the right things done. Start each day by identifying your most time-sensitive and important tasks. Create a plan that allows you to tackle those first, giving them your full attention without distraction. You'll not only be more productive but also less stressed, knowing that you're making real progress on what matters most.

The next time you feel tempted to multitask, pause. Take a deep breath, prioritize, and focus on completing one task at a time. You'll get more done, and you'll feel far more accomplished by the end of the day. Plus, with fewer mental juggling acts, you might even have more energy for the things you want to do, like spending time with your kids or finally finishing that book.

2.3 The Power of the To-Do List: Turning Chaos into Checkmarks

There's nothing quite like the magic of a to-do list. It's like transferring all the mental clutter, random "don't forgets," and nagging little tasks out of your brain and onto paper (or an app, for the digitally inclined). Not only does this free up valuable headspace, but it also gives you something deeply satisfying: a tangible list of all the stuff you've accomplished.

When we jot down tasks, especially those seemingly unmanageable "tankers," it's like unloading cargo. Suddenly, what once seemed overwhelming becomes organized. You're no longer juggling mental grenades; instead, you're working through each task, one satisfying checkmark at a time.

And here's the science part: every time you check something off that list, your brain releases a little hit of dopamine — one of the "feel-good" hormones. This is your brain's way of giving you a high-five, a tiny moment of "you did it!" It's the same rush you get from eating chocolate or finishing a workout, but here, it's the sweet taste of productivity.

By the end of the day, when you look back at all those checkmarks, you're not just seeing a list; you're seeing proof that, yes, you did get things done. That momentum builds confidence, reduces stress, and boosts your mood, reinforcing your ability to tackle tomorrow's list with the same level of badassery.

So, here's the takeaway: make to-do lists your daily ritual. Don't aim for perfection; just aim to move forward. Write down the essentials, knock them off, and let those little bursts of satisfaction propel you forward. Because sometimes, it's not about conquering the world in a day — it's about conquering your list, one dopamine-inducing checkmark at a time.

2.4. Knowing Your Worth (And Why You Shouldn't Install That Dishwasher)

You're a very capable woman. I mean, you've managed to juggle kids, work, relationships, and everything else life has thrown at you, so what's a little DIY project, right? But here's the thing—just because you can install a new dishwasher, rewire the house, or repaint the entire kitchen doesn't mean you should. Have you ever stopped to ask yourself what your time is worth? I'm talking dollars and cents here, people. Time to crunch some numbers.

You're a career-driven mom with an impressive skill set, so let's treat your time like the valuable commodity it is. What's your hourly rate at work? Go ahead, do the math. If your job pays $40 an hour, and it's going to take you four hours, three YouTube tutorials, and two trips to Home Depot to install that dishwasher, well, you've just blown $160 worth of your own time—not to mention a good chunk of your sanity. And let's be honest, the dishwasher will probably leak anyway.

Now, imagine instead you pay someone $100 to install it for you. Sure, it feels like a hit to your wallet, but guess what? You've just saved yourself time, energy, and probably a few curse words. Plus, you now have those four hours back to spend on something that actually brings you joy—or at the very least, something less painful than crouching under your sink with a wrench.

But it's not just about the money. Let's factor in something equally important: fun. Or rather, the total absence of it. Because sure, you could install the dishwasher, but does that sound like a good time? Are you the kind of person who finds joy in being elbows-deep in plumbing, or would you rather use those four hours for, say, getting coffee with a friend, catching up on your favorite show, or maybe just enjoying some peace and quiet for once?

The point is, knowing your worth isn't just about recognizing your professional value—it's about valuing your time in all aspects of life. Sometimes the smartest decision isn't doing something yourself just because you're capable of it, but rather outsourcing the tasks that drain your energy (and your patience). Think of it like delegating at work. You wouldn't do every little task in the office if it made more sense to pass it off, right? Same goes for home.

It's also important to recognize that time saved is money saved in the long run. If paying someone else to do that task means you get to spend time on something that energizes you, reduces your stress, or allows you to be more present for your kids, then that's money well spent. It's not about being wasteful—it's about investing in yourself.

So next time you find yourself contemplating whether to tackle that giant task yourself, ask yourself three questions:

1. What's my hourly rate?

2. How much will this task cost in time, effort, and potential mental breakdowns?

3. Would I rather spend that time doing literally anything else?

If the answer is yes, call the professional. Pay the fee. Then pour yourself a cup of coffee (or a glass of wine) and relax, knowing that your time was far better spent. Because knowing your worth isn't just about your paycheck—it's about understanding when your energy is better used for things that actually bring value to your life.

Not installing that dishwasher? That's priceless.

Time management as a working mom isn't about packing your calendar full and running yourself ragged. It's about being smart with your energy, setting boundaries, and remembering that sometimes, less is more. Planning and prioritizing are key—focus on the important tasks that truly move the needle for you and your family. Instead of trying to be everywhere at once, be selective about what fills your time.

It's okay (actually, it's more than okay) to say "no" to events, commitments, and activities that don't serve you or that leave you feeling overwhelmed. You don't need to be busy to be valuable. And just because you can do something yourself doesn't mean you should. Call in reinforcements when needed, whether that's outsourcing tasks or enlisting help from others.

At the end of the day, it's not about how much you get done—it's about being present and putting your energy where it matters most. Embrace the power of thoughtful planning, protect your peace, and don't be afraid to take the load off when you need to. You've got this!

CHAPTER 3

Parenting as a Process (AKA Herding Cats)

3.1. The Power of Routines (and Why You Should Stack 'Em Like Pancakes)

If there's one secret weapon in the wild world of parenting, it's routines. Routines are the unsung heroes of sanity—whether we're talking about meal times, bedtimes, or just trying to get the kids into the car without a full-blown negotiation that would make a diplomat sweat. And guess what? It's not just you who thrives on structure—kids, toddlers, and even babies are all about routines. Like most adults, they function best when they know exactly what's expected. Turns out, it's a lot easier to get through the day when the whole household isn't winging it.

Now, before you roll your eyes at the idea of being that organized, let me introduce you to something even more magical: habit stacking. It's as efficient as it sounds and as life-saving as it gets. The idea is simple—group a bunch of small habits together so they happen seamlessly, one after another, like a domino effect. Think of it like assembling the perfect breakfast sandwich but for your daily routines.

For example, let's talk about the morning rush. Instead of flying around trying to find shoes, brushing teeth, packing lunches, and getting out the door (all while losing your mind), you can habit stack this process to make it almost smooth. Start with something simple, like laying out clothes the night before (that's habit one). Follow it up with packing lunches right after dinner (habit two), and leave the backpacks by the door (habit three). Suddenly, your mornings go from chaotic to (mostly) calm because everything happens in a predictable, repeatable order. And no, you won't be searching for that missing shoe at 8 a.m. while shouting "We're late!"

Bedtime? Same thing. It's all about setting the tone. Bath time leads to brushing teeth, which leads to story time, which leads to lights out. The routine is predictable, everyone knows what's next, and the end result is a smoother (dare I say, quieter?) transition to bedtime. Even the wildest toddlers eventually pick up on these signals, and suddenly, you're not spending an hour trying to convince them that yes, they do need to sleep.

And don't even get me started on getting into the car. Instead of wrangling kids one by one while they scatter like free-range chickens, make it part of the routine. Shoes on, jackets on, bags in hand, then everyone lines up like it's a parade, ready to march into the vehicle. Habit stack it—shoes, then jackets, then bags, then the glorious moment when you lock the doors and no one can escape.

But routines aren't just about avoiding chaos—they also give kids a sense of security. When they know what to expect, they feel more in control, even if they're not the ones calling the shots. And you? You get to feel like a parenting ninja who's one step ahead of the game (at least most of the time).

So, embrace the power of routines. Stack your habits like pancakes. And watch as the small, predictable rhythms of your day help you turn the circus into something that almost looks like a well-oiled machine.

3.2. Delegation: Raising Future Adults, Not Just Kids

Let's talk about one of the best-kept secrets of parenting: delegation. You see, somewhere along the way, we got this idea that being a "good" mom means doing everything ourselves—every single thing—from the laundry to the lunches to managing the family's entire social calendar. But here's the truth: being a great mom actually means raising future adults, not just kids. And guess what? Adults do chores. Adults manage tasks. Adults help. So, why not start early and let your kids take some of that load off your plate?

Enter the magic of delegation. As your kids grow and their capacity to handle responsibility increases, it's time to start shifting some of the day-to-day work onto their little (or not-so-little) shoulders. Think of it like running a mini organization, with you as the CEO and them as your increasingly competent junior staff. And the best part? You get to use the power of situational leadership—adapting your leadership style based on their development stage—to help them learn and grow into these new roles.

Here's how it works: when your kids are young, you're in the Directive phase of leadership. You're basically giving step-by-step instructions for everything. "Here's how we fold the laundry," "This is how you set the table," or "We brush our teeth before bed, not after breakfast." You're teaching them the ropes, and they need a lot of guidance because, well, they're still figuring out how to be humans.

As they get older and more capable, you can move into the Coaching phase. Now, instead of doing everything for them, you're offering more support and encouragement while letting them take the lead on certain tasks. "Hey, I saw you started folding the laundry. Let me show you a trick to make it faster." You're there to offer feedback, but they're starting to own their tasks.

Then comes the Supporting phase. At this stage, they've pretty much got it down, but they still need a little encouragement. You're delegating tasks like "Can you make dinner tonight?" or "Handle the grocery list for the week." They're more independent now, and you're stepping back while keeping an eye on things just to make sure it's all going smoothly.

Finally, when they've totally mastered a skill, you hit the Delegating phase, a.k.a. your parenting nirvana. This is when you can confidently hand off the task and trust that it'll get done without your involvement. "Oh, the dishwasher is already loaded and running? Wonderful." "You remembered your practice schedule and got your gear packed? Amazing." At this stage, they're practically running their own lives, and you can take a step back, sip your coffee, and bask in the glow of knowing you're raising self-sufficient humans.

Delegation isn't just about getting help with household chores—it's about teaching your kids life skills they'll need as adults. You're not just assigning tasks; you're giving them the opportunity to grow, build confidence, and learn responsibility. Plus, the earlier they start learning these skills, the easier the transition to adulthood will be. Trust me, future-you will be thankful when your teenager can handle their own laundry and actually remember to pack their own lunch.

So, the next time you feel overwhelmed by the sheer amount of stuff that needs to get done, pause and think: "Can I delegate this?" Your kids are far more capable than they might seem, and as they get older, they should be contributing more. Not only does it lighten your load, but it also prepares them for the big wide world out there. Plus, there's no better feeling than realizing that you're not just managing chaos—you're raising competent, capable, future adults who can handle their business.

And who knows? Maybe one day, they'll even delegate something back to you. Now that's leadership!

3.3. Older Siblings to the Rescue: The Homework Hack You Didn't Know You Needed

Ah, homework time—also known as that magical hour when everyone suddenly needs your undivided attention, and you're left feeling like a human Google search engine. But before you resign yourself to another night of geometry problems and spelling tests, let's talk about one of the most underrated parenting hacks out there: the older sibling assist.

That's right, if you've got an older child, you've been sitting on a goldmine of homework help. Letting an older sibling help a younger one with their schoolwork is a win-win for everyone involved—and it's not just because you get a breather from deciphering new math. There's a ton of brain-boosting, confidence-building goodness packed into this strategy for both kids.

For the older sibling, it's a chance to flex their intellectual muscles. Research shows that teaching others is one of the best ways to reinforce learning. When your older child explains something to their younger sibling—whether it's basic math, reading, or science—they're essentially relearning and solidifying those concepts themselves. They're recalling information, breaking it down, and presenting it in a way that makes sense to their younger sibling. It's like studying, but without the flashcards, and it helps them lock in what they know even more deeply. Plus, they get to feel like the expert, which is always a confidence boost. Who doesn't want to feel like the wise big sibling who's got it all figured out?

Then there's the leadership angle. When an older sibling steps in to help, they're not just sharing knowledge—they're taking on a role of responsibility. They're showing patience, empathy, and a sense of duty. That's a powerful feeling for any kid. You're basically handing them a cape and saying, "You've got this." Suddenly, your older child transforms into a mini mentor, building not only their confidence but also their sense of pride in being able to help their younger sibling succeed.

For the younger sibling, it's a whole different ball game. Having their older brother or sister help with homework can be way less intimidating than asking a parent (or a teacher). There's something about sibling teamwork that makes learning feel less like a chore and more like a shared adventure. The younger one gets to feel supported by someone they look up to—someone who's been where they are and understands the struggle. It fosters a sense of closeness between siblings, turning homework time into an opportunity for connection instead of frustration.

Now, will this always go smoothly? Of course not. Expect a few eye rolls, sighs, and the occasional "That's not how my teacher does it!" But overall, you're creating an environment where learning becomes a family effort, and both kids get something valuable out of the experience.

And let's not forget the bonus: by letting the older sibling step in, you free up some time and mental space for yourself. Whether it's squeezing in five minutes of peace with a cup of tea or getting a head start on dinner, having your kids help each other can give you that much-needed break from the endless to-do list.

So next time you're faced with the nightly homework shuffle, consider delegating the task to your in-house tutor. You'll be surprised how much both kids benefit—academically, emotionally, and maybe even socially (cue the occasional sibling bonding moment). Plus, you get the satisfaction of watching your older child step up, take charge, and reinforce their own learning while giving their younger sibling a helping hand.

Who knew homework time could turn into a lesson in leadership and teamwork? Now, that's some extra credit right there!

3.4. Lead by Example: Because Nobody Wants to Mop While You're Eating Bonbons

Nothing grinds a kid's gears quite like being told to mop the floor while the rest of the household lounges around as if they're starring in a bonbon commercial. Can you blame them? We all know that the fastest way to breed mutiny on the household chore ship is to bark orders while you're sinking into the couch with a snack in hand. If you want your kids to pitch in, it's time to step up and show them that you're all in this together. That's right—it's time to lead by example.

The truth is, leadership in parenting isn't about delegating tasks while you relax like a queen on her throne (although, yes, that sounds amazing). It's about rolling up your sleeves, getting your hands dirty, and showing your kids that the house doesn't magically clean itself. When they see you wiping down counters or scrubbing the bathroom, it sends a powerful message: we're all responsible for keeping this place running. You're modeling the behavior you want to see, and believe it or not, they're paying attention—even if they pretend not to.

Leading by example isn't just about fairness, though. It's also about teaching your kids what good work ethic looks like. You're showing them that no one is above the daily grind, not even you. And while you're at it, you're giving them a front-row seat to what teamwork looks like. Instead of saying, "Go clean your room while I sit here and relax," you're saying, "Let's tackle this together." Suddenly, it feels a little less like punishment and a little more like shared responsibility. After all, if Mom is scrubbing the stove and Dad's vacuuming the living room, it's kind of hard for the kids to argue their way out of dusting the shelves.

Plus, there's a hidden bonus here: it's a bonding opportunity. When you all chip in together, even the most mundane tasks can turn into something a bit more fun (or at least tolerable). Turn on some music, turn up the volume, and make it a team effort. Before you know it, everyone's singing along to whatever catchy tune is playing while cleaning up the house. You'll be amazed at how much faster the chores get done—and how much less grumbling there is—when it feels like a group activity.

And here's the kicker: by leading by example, you're setting the foundation for habits that will (hopefully) stick with your kids long after they've flown the nest. They're learning that keeping a tidy house isn't someone else's job. It's not a task reserved for the "chore fairy" (who is just you in disguise). It's something everyone does, and when they grow up, they'll (ideally) carry that sense of responsibility into their own homes. So, not only are you getting help now, but you're setting them up for a future of less mess and more personal accountability. Parenting win!

Now, does this mean you can never take a break while your kids do chores? Of course not! Once the example is set and everyone's on board, feel free to occasionally prop up your feet while they knock out a few tasks. But in those early days—or whenever a chore revolt seems imminent—remember that the sight of you pitching in alongside them is often the key to keeping morale high.

After all, no one likes feeling like Cinderella while everyone else is living their best royal life. So, swap the bonbons for a broom now and then, and watch as the household chore dynamic shifts in your favor. Leading by example isn't just good for the floors—it's good for the whole family.

CHAPTER 4

Money Matters (Make Your Paycheck Stretch Like Elastic)

4.1. The Budget Breakdown: Because Even Socrates Would Want You to Track Your Spending

Ah, budgets. Not exactly the most fun topic, but essential, especially when there are family expenses, extracurriculars, and an endless parade of school projects that seem to appear out of nowhere. The trick here isn't just to have a budget—it's to understand where your money's actually going, much like our philosopher friend Socrates might advise. After all, if "the unexamined life is not worth living," then surely the unexamined budget isn't worth spending.

Think about it: When was the last time you looked at your spending? Socrates would probably suggest that a closer examination might reveal a few things. That daily drive-through coffee? Those "I swear it's educational" toy purchases? Maybe even the subscription for that one streaming service no one actually watches? They all add up, and without checking in on where your cash is flowing, it's easy to get lost.

Assessing Spending, Socratic-Style

Step back and ask yourself some good old "Socratic" questions about your budget:

- Where's the money going, and is it making my life better?

- Is there a purchase that's just not serving the greater good (or at least, your grocery budget)?

- If someone else examined my spending, would I feel embarrassed explaining a line item or two? (Hello, impulse buys!)

Finding the Balance

Budgeting doesn't have to be an all-or-nothing affair. Maybe it's more about swapping what doesn't matter as much (those dusty memberships) for what does bring joy or value to your family. The occasional splurge is okay, but knowing what's really worth it will help you make conscious choices. It's about crafting a life you actually want—one that's sustainable and thoughtful rather than reactive.

Taking Stock with Humor and Grace

Budgeting doesn't mean you have to morph into a super-frugal minimalist overnight. Start small, check in regularly, and let your spending reflect your family's unique priorities. When you understand where your money's going, you'll feel more in control, and maybe even a bit liberated.

In the end, Socrates would be proud: You're examining your budget and your life—one line item at a time. And who knows, maybe that examined budget will help you afford a little something extra, guilt-free.

4.2. More Money, More Problems: Knowing When to Chase the Promotion and When to Politely Pass

Ah, promotions—the sweet promise of more money, prestige, and maybe even a better parking spot. But before you throw yourself into the late-night grind for that shiny new title, let's talk about the hidden truth Biggie Smalls taught us: more money often means more problems.

Sure, more money is tempting, but it often comes with strings attached. That bigger paycheck might mean sacrificing evenings, weekends, and possibly your sanity to meet new demands. So, how do you know when to chase the promotion or politely back away and keep your life (mostly) your own?

When to Hit Pause on the Promotion Train

If the promotion would come at the cost of everything you love outside of work—like having dinner with your family, or occasionally knowing what the inside of your house looks like—then it's worth considering a hard pass. There's a big difference between working with your family in mind and working so much you never see them.

Ask yourself these key questions:

- Will the extra income improve my life right now, or will it just end up funding late-night takeout and an extra bottle of eye cream?

- Do I actually want this role, or am I more interested in the paycheck that comes with it?

- Will I still feel human with this new workload, or will I morph into a zombie in a blazer?

When to Embrace the Grind (for a While)

On the flip side, sometimes grinding through a tougher job now can lead to some serious perks down the road. If you're looking at a clear path to a dream role, a long-term financial goal, or just getting a bit ahead, a little hustle can be worth it. But think of it as a strategic sprint, not a permanent marathon.

If you're ready to take on more and the late nights won't turn you into a frazzled mom doing sleep-deprived lunchbox prep, the promotion might be worth it. Set a timeline for how long you're willing to hustle at this level and keep an eye on how it's impacting you and your family.

The Balancing Act of the Century

In the end, know that a job should work for you, not the other way around. When it's all said and done, remember that the payoff is a life that feels fulfilling—not just a paycheck that requires you to sacrifice everything else. Decide where you're willing to put in extra effort, and where you'll draw the line. Because more money is great, but a life where you're actually around to spend it? Now that's priceless.

CHAPTER 5

Knowing Your Team

5.1. Building Trust: The Honest (and Humble) Way to Parenting

One of the most important things you can build with your children—besides a LEGO tower that somehow always ends up underfoot—is trust. And like any sturdy structure, trust takes time, effort, and the occasional humble admission that you don't always have it all figured out.

Being honest with your kids, even when it's tough, is the foundation for strong communication and lasting trust. They need to know that they can come to you with their problems, their fears, and even their mistakes without fear of judgment. But here's the catch—you've got to model that honesty yourself. That means admitting when you've messed up, owning your mistakes, and yes, even apologizing to your kids when you've been wrong.

Nobody likes to admit they've blown it—especially not to their children. But here's the thing—kids tend to be a lot more forgiving of our mistakes than adults. They're surprisingly compassionate, and when you own up to something, they'll usually respond with grace and understanding. It's like they have an internal radar for fairness, and when they see you making an effort to fix things, they're right there with you, ready to forgive and move on.

That said, kids don't come out of the womb fully grasping all the pressures and challenges you're up against as a parent. It takes time for them to develop that understanding. So while they're quick to forgive, they might not always see why you're stressed or overwhelmed unless you take the time to explain. It's okay to let them in on some of the "grown-up" struggles—not in a way that burdens them, but in a way that gives them context. Maybe they didn't realize you had a huge work deadline or that you were running on three hours of sleep. Being transparent about what's going on in your world helps them understand that you're human too, and sometimes, things get messy.

Keeping the lines of communication open is just as important. Encourage your kids to talk to you about anything—whether it's something big, like a school issue, or something small, like what they dreamed about last night. The more you listen without judgment, the more they'll feel comfortable coming to you when it matters most. And when those tough conversations do happen, be honest, even if the answer isn't what they want to hear. Kids are sharp—they can sense when you're giving them the runaround. Being upfront shows them that you respect their feelings and their ability to handle the truth.

Of course, trust isn't built in a day. It's built over time, through consistent communication and those small moments of honesty. So, when the inevitable parenting mistake happens (because it will happen), take a deep breath, apologize, and keep that conversation going. It's not about being perfect—it's about being real. And your kids will appreciate that far more than any perfect façade you could ever maintain.

5.2. Filling the Love Bucket: Speaking Your Child's Love Language

If there's one universal truth to parenting, it's this: every kid is unique in how they give and receive love. Trying to connect with them without understanding their "love language" is like trying to fill a piggy bank with confetti—you're putting in the effort, but it's not adding up where it counts. Just like adults, kids have their own way of feeling loved, and tapping into that can make a world of difference in your connection with them.

Enter the concept of The Five Love Languages. Developed by Dr. Gary Chapman, the five love languages are: Words of Affirmation, Acts of Service, Receiving Gifts, Quality Time, and Physical Touch. Each child has one or two love languages that fill their "love bucket"—or think of it as their emotional bank account. When you "make a deposit" in a way that resonates with them, you're adding to their reserves of love and security. But if you're using the wrong "currency," it's like handing them Monopoly money—it doesn't hold the same value for them.

For example, let's say your child's love language is Quality Time. You might think you're showing love by showering them with gifts, but in their mind, you're tossing pennies in an empty well. What they want is for you to sit down and play their favorite board game or go on a little adventure together. For them, that's a million-dollar deposit, while the toy car is a nice gesture but barely registers on the emotional balance sheet.

Or maybe your child feels loved through Words of Affirmation. When they bring home a school project, they don't want a new LEGO set—they want to hear you gush about how smart and creative they are. They're not looking for a grand gesture; they just need to know that you see their efforts and are proud of them. That verbal boost? It's like adding bonus interest to their love account.

Now, understanding this can also be helpful when it comes to "withdrawals." Kids understand when you've had to take time, energy, or focus away—sometimes they feel it like a little deduction in their emotional bank account. The key is to recognize this and balance it with thoughtful "deposits" that they truly value.

So how do you find out your child's love language? Observe what makes them light up the most. Do they cling to you for hugs (Physical Touch)? Do they beam when you thank them for helping (Words of Affirmation)? Pay attention to what they ask for repeatedly—that's usually a big clue.

Once you've cracked their love language, you'll know exactly what kind of deposits to make to keep their emotional bank account thriving. And the best part? When they feel loved in a way that speaks to them, they're more confident, more resilient, and, a lot happier. So go ahead—figure out what fills their love bucket, and watch their little hearts overflow.

5.3. Knowing Your Kid's Personality: Birth Order and Beyond

If you've ever wondered why one child seems to instinctively take charge while another is a natural peacekeeper, you're not alone. The secret sauce behind these tendencies might just be in their birth order. Alfred Adler, a pioneering psychologist, explored the idea that the order in which a child is born shapes certain personality traits. Adler's theory suggests that your firstborn, middle child, youngest, or only child might come pre-packaged with distinct personality tendencies that shape how they relate to the world (and, let's face it, to each other).

Now, this isn't a hard science—there's always room for individuality—but birth order can give you some helpful insights. Let's dive into each spot in the sibling lineup and see what Adler thought might come with the territory:

The Firstborn: The Responsible Leader

Firstborns often take on a natural sense of responsibility. They tend to be reliable, organized, and high achievers—think of them as the "mini grown-ups" of the family. They're usually the ones who follow rules and often feel responsible for their younger siblings. Adler believed that firstborns strive to live up to the expectations set for them, sometimes making them more anxious about perfection or achievement. So if you've got a little leader on your hands, giving them opportunities to take responsibility in ways they enjoy (without the pressure of perfection) can make all the difference.

The Middle Child: The Diplomat and Peacemaker

Ah, the classic "middle child syndrome" might actually have some roots in psychology. According to Adler, middle children often become great negotiators and peacemakers. Sandwiched between the trailblazing firstborn and the attention grabbing youngest, they tend to be adaptable and sociable. Middle kids are often skilled at compromise, and they can be both independent and diplomatic. Just remember that middle children sometimes feel overlooked, so making one-on-one time for them is like depositing directly into their "I'm seen" account.

The Youngest: The Free Spirit

The youngest child often benefits from the fact that by the time they come along, parents are a bit more relaxed (or just plain tired). Adler believed that youngest children grow up with a sense of freedom and a natural flair for attention. They can be charming, outgoing, and often a bit of a rule-breaker. They're typically the comedians, the dreamers, and sometimes, the ones who push boundaries just to see what happens. Since they're used to having older siblings do things for them, building independence and responsibility is a great focus for these little adventurers.

The Only Child: The Lone Ranger

Only children have their own unique personality profile. Often, they develop mature traits early on, as they're mostly interacting with adults. Adler suggested that only children can be detail-oriented, conscientious, and often quite comfortable being alone. They're usually self-sufficient, but sometimes, they can feel like the whole world is on their shoulders. Social interactions with other kids their age can help balance out the grown-up vibe they might adopt early on.

Why Knowing Birth Order Can Help You Connect

Understanding these personality tendencies can help you not only connect with each child but also tailor your approach to meet them where they are. Maybe your responsible firstborn thrives with clear structure, while your youngest lights up with a little extra freedom to be themselves. Your middle child might respond best to affirmations of their unique value, while an only child appreciates your respect for their independence. It's like having a "cheat sheet" to help fill their emotional bank account in ways that resonate.

These are just tendencies—not set-in-stone rules. Each child is a unique mix of traits, interests, and quirks. But if birth order helps you see why one of your kids is the planner and another is the comedian, embrace it! It's all part of the fun and complexity of getting to know each of them as they are. And remember, your understanding and appreciation of their individual quirks and strengths? That's a priceless deposit in each of their love buckets.

5.4. Discipline: When to Use the Carrot (or the Stick)

Discipline in a multi-kid household is like navigating a minefield made of Legos—what works beautifully for one child could completely backfire with another. If only there were a one-size-fits-all approach to parenting, right? But alas, each of your little angels comes with their own unique temperament, preferences, and triggers. So, the question becomes: how do you know when to break out the carrot (aka the reward) or the stick (aka the consequence), and how do you tailor it to each child's specific needs?

First off, let's acknowledge that the whole carrot vs. stick thing is an age-old balancing act, and it's not about being overly soft or harsh—it's about being strategic. You don't want your home to be a free-for-all where everyone's running wild, but you also don't want to turn into a drill sergeant barking orders. The magic lies in knowing which approach works for each kid, at which moment, and for what behavior.

Here's the trick: what motivates one child may not motivate another, and what feels like a reward to one might feel like a punishment to someone else. For example, your oldest child might live for screen time and see any reduction in that time as a fate worse than death. Meanwhile, your middle child might be indifferent to screens but would crumble at the thought of losing dessert privileges for a week. Your youngest? They may view even the suggestion of an early bedtime as cruel and unusual punishment. The point is, you've got to know what makes each kid tick.

The Carrot: Rewarding the Wins

Let's start with the carrot because, let's face it, positive reinforcement is a lot more fun (for both you and the kids). Using rewards isn't about bribing your kids to behave, but rather reinforcing good behavior by attaching something positive to it. For some kids, this could be extra time doing something they love—whether it's playing video games, staying up a bit later, or getting to pick what's for dinner. For others, it could be earning privileges like a sleepover or even something as simple as a sticker on a chart.

The key is to find out what makes each child's eyes light up. Maybe one kid works hard for the promise of a new toy, while another just wants to hear you say how proud you are of them. There's no one-size-fits-all carrot; you have to customize it based on what genuinely motivates each child. And remember: the reward doesn't have to be material. Often, extra one-on-one time with you or getting to choose the family movie can be just as valuable (and much easier on your wallet).

But here's where it gets tricky: once your kids get the hang of the carrot, you don't want to overuse it. If every little task they complete comes with a reward, you're setting yourself up for a future where they won't lift a finger unless there's a prize waiting for them. Instead, focus on using rewards to reinforce bigger wins—helping them develop habits, stick to routines, or make good choices over time.

The Stick: When Consequences Are Necessary

Now, let's talk about the stick. Sometimes, no matter how many carrots you dangle, the behavior just isn't cutting it, and consequences are necessary. But here's the catch: the stick only works if it's actually meaningful to the child in question. If you take away something they don't care about, it's not a punishment—it's just a minor inconvenience. And worse, they'll learn nothing from it.

Take, for instance, your kid who doesn't care about screens but would be devastated to miss their soccer practice. If they're pushing boundaries or breaking the rules, a consequence that impacts their social or physical activities will hit harder than losing their tablet for a few days. Conversely, for the child who's attached to their devices, limiting screen time could be the exact motivation they need to rethink their actions.

It's also important to keep consequences tied to the behavior in a logical way. If your kid made a mess in the living room and refused to clean it up, the stick could be losing their free time until the mess is cleaned. If they've been rude or disrespectful, missing out on something fun (like dessert or a playdate) can reinforce the idea that kindness and respect lead to more positive outcomes.

Know Your Audience: Customizing Your Response

Discipline is like a game of chess—you have to think a few steps ahead and know your opponent's next move. Some kids respond well to reason and explanation, while others need a firm boundary. But the biggest lesson here is that no two kids are the same. One might be crushed by the thought of missing out on a reward, while another might take a consequence as a personal challenge and dig their heels in deeper. You have to be flexible enough to adapt your approach based on who you're dealing with and what's going on at the moment.

The beauty of understanding your kids' individual motivations is that you can start shaping their behavior in a way that feels natural to them. You'll know when it's time to offer the carrot for a job well done and when it's time to pull out the stick to steer them back on course. And as your kids grow, their triggers and rewards will shift, which means you'll need to adjust your tactics too.

Discipline is not a "set it and forget it" situation. As your kids grow older, what worked to motivate or correct them at age 5 is not going to cut it when they're 12. That's why constant feedback is crucial. You need to regularly check in, observe, and adjust your approach as their interests, motivators, and sense of independence evolve.

Remember, the toy that used to spark joy might now be replaced by social activities or extra phone time. The punishment that once sent them into sulk mode might not even faze them anymore. This is where your flexibility as a parent comes into play. Just like in a job, you wouldn't expect the same incentives and consequences to work for a teenager as they would for a preschooler. So why would parenting be any different?

This is where ongoing feedback loops become your best friend. Talk to your kids, observe their reactions, and be willing to pivot when something stops working. Maybe your 8-year-old responds well to verbal praise, but your teenager couldn't care less unless it's tied to freedom or autonomy. Keep tabs on what lights them up and what they value. Discipline isn't just about correcting behavior; it's about helping them grow—and that's an ongoing process.

Discipline isn't about controlling your kids—it's about guiding them. It's a dance between motivation and correction, rewards and consequences, all while being flexible enough to adapt as they grow. And with constant feedback, you're not just reacting to bad behavior—you're proactively helping shape better choices.

5.5. Identifying Your "Mom Triggers" Before the Meltdown

Parenting is a mix of love, joy, and…stress triggers. We all have those specific situations that make us feel like we're seconds away from a "mommy meltdown." Whether it's a messy kitchen first thing in the morning, kids bickering at full volume, or the looming to-do list that never seems to end, everyone has their personal tipping points. The trick is learning what your triggers are so you can handle them before they turn into a full-blown mom-meltdown moment.

Understanding what pushes your buttons is all about knowing yourself better. It might take some reflection (and a few deep breaths), but taking note of these triggers will pay off in ways you can feel daily.

What Are Your Triggers?

Think about your most frustrating moments. Is it the state of the house? The sound of whining? An overflowing schedule? Once you've pinpointed your triggers, you can start to plan ahead, setting up systems or mental notes to sidestep a meltdown before it happens.

Strategies for Heading Off a Meltdown

- Practice Mindful Breaks: If you know mornings are stressful, set aside even five minutes to breathe, sip coffee, or prepare your mental game plan before things get chaotic.

- Adjust Expectations: For some moms, the urge to keep everything perfect can be a huge trigger. Remember, it's okay if everything doesn't go according to plan. Sometimes, "good enough" is exactly what everyone needs.

- Delegate or Set Boundaries: If constant demands on your time and energy are wearing you down, say "no" where you can and ask for help where it's possible. Kids old enough to pitch in? Let them take on a task or two.

The Power of a Self-Care Pause

Before things reach critical mass, sometimes you just need a moment to yourself. A few deep breaths, a five-minute break, or even a quick walk outside can be all it takes to reset.

Know When to Laugh

Finally, remember that humor is one of the best tools in your mom toolkit. Sometimes, embracing the chaos with a little laugh and knowing that everyone has their tough days can keep a meltdown from hitting hard.

Knowing yourself and your limits helps you set boundaries and expectations that protect your sanity. Because when you're calm and collected, your family feels it, too—and everyone benefits.

CHAPTER 6

Self-Care: It's Not a Myth, But It May Involve Wine

6.1. Self-Care: The Art of Occasionally Choosing Yourself

Let's get one thing straight: self-care is not about an elaborate spa day (though, if that's your thing, go for it). It's about intentionally choosing yourself—at least occasionally. Self-care isn't selfish. It's survival. In a world where your time and energy are constantly being divvied up between work, kids, school projects, laundry, and grocery runs, finding time for yourself can feel like trying to locate a matching sock in a sea of mismatched ones. You wouldn't let your phone battery drop to zero and then expect it to power your life, right? So why do we treat our own energy reserves that way? You need to recharge, You only get one battery aka one body, one mind, one you—so be kind to it.

And speaking of being kind to your body, let me tell you about my all-time favorite self-care ritual: cooking myself. Yes, I'm talking about cranking up the heat in a sauna or soaking in a super hot bath until I feel like a slow-roasting human casserole. There's just something about turning your core temperature up to "sweat mode" that feels like a reset button for your brain. And it's not just for the immediate relaxation—the science behind it is solid. Turns out, raising your core temperature triggers a whole host of health benefits like boosting circulation, reducing stress, and releasing magical little things called heat shock proteins. These proteins help repair your body's cells, which makes me feel like a rejuvenated superhero (even if I still have to face Mount Laundry afterward).

So when you think about self-care, whether it's a leisurely bath or a trip to the sauna, remember that it's not just an indulgence—it's maintenance. Like oil changes for a car, you've got to give yourself that time to recharge. And if I'm going to be stuck in the chaos of life, I might as well do it feeling warm, relaxed, and as close to a human sauna roll as possible.

Here's the kicker: dedicate white space in your calendar for these moments. Just because your day has a free hour doesn't mean you need to fill it with errands or meetings. Sometimes, that empty slot should be reserved for filling a super-sized cup of self-care. And yes, that means guilt-free time to yourself. So, whether it's turning up the heat or something else that fills your cup, make sure you're taking time to choose yourself—you deserve it.

So, go ahead, pencil yourself into your own schedule. Your future self will thank you.

6.2. Mom Guilt: The Uninvited Guest That Never Leaves

Ah, mom guilt—that nagging voice in the back of your head reminding you that no matter what you're doing, it's never enough. If you're at work, you feel guilty for not being home with the kids. If you're home with the kids, you feel guilty for not working harder or advancing your career. And if by some miracle you've carved out time for yourself, well, cue the full-blown guilt-fest for daring to relax. It's like the annoying houseguest who refuses to take a hint and leave.

But here's the thing: mom guilt is a liar. It tells you that you're falling short, but the reality is, you're doing your best—and your best is more than enough. Kids don't need perfect moms; they need happy moms, moms who show up, do their best, and occasionally mess up. Because let's face it, nobody gets this whole parenting thing 100% right. We're all winging it with a coffee in one hand and a forgotten permission slip in the other.

The tricky part about mom guilt is that it sneaks up on you when you least expect it. Maybe it's after you missed a school event because of a work deadline, or perhaps it's when you handed the kids an iPad instead of crafting an elaborate educational activity. The guilt doesn't care what triggered it—it just shows up and starts throwing a party.

You can't do everything. And that's okay. You're juggling more than most, and sometimes, one ball is going to drop. It's part of the process. What matters most is how you show your kids that life isn't about perfection—it's about effort, love, and balance. Teaching them that it's okay to make mistakes is one of the greatest lessons you can give.

Next time mom guilt tries to creep in, remind yourself: you're raising human beings, not crafting robots. Imperfection is part of the deal, and those "less-than-perfect" moments are where the magic often happens.

Mom guilt often doesn't just come from within—it gets a major boost from the opinions, comments, and unsolicited judgments of others. Family members, especially, can be expert guilt-trippers, whether they mean to or not. Maybe it's the offhand remark from an aunt about how in her day she didn't need screens to keep kids entertained. Or maybe it's the passive-aggressive comment from a well-meaning relative who "just doesn't understand" why you can't make it to every family gathering.

You can't let those judgments get to you. Other people—even family—don't get a say in how you choose to balance work, motherhood, and your own sanity. They don't know the ins and outs of your daily life, and they definitely don't get to dictate how you spend your time or energy.

When you're already feeling the weight of mom guilt, it's easy to let someone else's comments send you spiraling. But here's your reminder: no one else is living your life. They don't understand the deadlines you're juggling, the sleepless nights, or the 37 mental tabs you have open at any given time. So why should their opinions hold so much power?

The key is to develop a filter for this kind of noise. When those comments come rolling in, remind yourself that their judgment is not a reflection of your reality. If someone makes you feel less than for how you're doing things, that's their problem, not yours. You know your priorities, you know what works for your family, and at the end of the day, the only people whose opinions truly matter are the ones under your roof.

Next time a family member pipes up with their two cents, smile, nod, and politely throw that opinion in the mental "thanks, but no thanks" bin. You've got bigger things to focus on—like being the best mom you can be, not the mom someone else thinks you should be.

6.3. Asking for Help: Building Your Support Squad

Every parent eventually learns: you can't do it all on your own. Whether it's because the baby hasn't slept in days, you're swamped with work, or you just need a mental break, there's no shame in asking for help. In fact, it's one of the smartest things you can do. Leaning on a support system doesn't make you any less capable—it makes you human.

Think of it as assembling your personal "support squad." Friends, family, coworkers, mom groups, or even a trusted therapist can be the lifelines you need to make it through those challenging days. Each member of your squad brings something different to the table, and together, they can provide the encouragement, advice, or even just the friendly distraction you need.

Friends and Family: The First Responder Support

Friends who've been through similar challenges are a treasure. They understand the struggle, can offer empathy (and maybe some humor), and can even jump in with practical help if they're nearby. Sometimes, all you need is a quick coffee catch-up or a text thread full of inside jokes to reset and feel ready to tackle another day.

Coworkers: Your Everyday Allies

Let's face it—work doesn't pause for parenthood, but supportive coworkers can help bridge that gap. A quick vent session or a colleague who's willing to switch a shift when your kid's sick can make all the difference. Don't hesitate to let coworkers you trust know when you're juggling a bit too much; they're more understanding than we often give them credit for.

Mom Support Groups: Wisdom in Numbers

Support groups, whether in person or online, can be a parenting lifeline. There's something about hearing, "Yep, been there, done that" from other parents that immediately normalizes what you're going through. These groups offer practical tips, emotional support, and sometimes, just a place to vent where everyone gets it. From advice on sleep schedules to shared toddler tantrum tales, these spaces can give you real-world insights and a renewed sense of perspective.

Therapy: The Self-Care Strategy

Let's normalize this one: therapy is self-care. A therapist can offer an unbiased, professional perspective that can help you work through the stress and challenges of parenting. If you're carrying the weight of family, work, and personal goals, a therapist can provide strategies for managing stress, improving communication, and finding balance. It's an investment in both your mental health and your ability to show up for your kids.

Remember, asking for help isn't a sign of weakness; it's a sign of strength. There's no trophy for going it alone, but there is a lot of wisdom in building your own support system. Let people who care about you lighten the load, share the laughs, and give you that extra nudge when you need it most. Because in parenting—as in life—the journey is always better together.

6.4 Sometimes, You Get What You Pay For: The Case for Therapy

As much as family and friends want to help, there are times when venting to loved ones can feel like...well, a bit of a burden. Maybe it's that nagging feeling of guilt when you don't have a solution, or the worry that they're just giving you advice to cheer you up rather than to address what's really going on. And while talking with close friends and family is important, hiring a therapist can take a lot of that pressure off and give you a space where it's okay to unload—no strings attached.

When I decided to start working with a therapist, I quickly realized how freeing it was. No more guilt about taking up a friend's time, no need to worry that I'd be seen as a downer, and best of all, no bias. A therapist doesn't automatically take my side or jump to tell me what I want to hear. Instead, they help me dig into what's beneath the surface, guiding me to the root cause of issues. And because they're trained to help people navigate life's rough patches, their advice often goes beyond the well-meaning encouragement friends and family offer.

It turns out, investing in professional support can be a game-changer. Therapists are experts at helping you process your thoughts, understand your triggers, and uncover hidden patterns. And the best part? You walk away with strategies that you're more likely to put into action because they were developed without the influence of personal ties. They offer practical advice designed to work for you—not just to make you feel better in the moment.

Finding the right therapist is a bit like finding the perfect pair of shoes: you might need to try a few on before you find the one that actually fits. Not every therapist is going to be your style, and that's okay. Some might feel too stiff, some too soft, and others just don't quite fit your vibe. But with patience and a few tries, you're likely to find one who's just right for you.

Just like with shoes, it's worth putting in the time to find a therapist who feels comfortable and supportive in the way you need. Sometimes, you'll click right away, and other times, it might take a few sessions to know if they're the right fit. And if one isn't right, moving on is absolutely okay. Just like you wouldn't buy shoes that pinch, you don't have to settle for a therapist who doesn't quite "get" you.

When you finally find the right one, it makes all the difference. A therapist who fits will understand your struggles, offer insights that feel meaningful, and guide you in a way that resonates. That's when you know you're getting exactly what you need, and the journey ahead feels just a little bit easier.

In the end, finding someone to talk to without the worry of burdening them, who's also equipped to help you grow, is invaluable. Sometimes, what you pay for is exactly what you need to feel stronger, lighter, and ready to tackle life with a clearer mind.

6.5. Cuddle Power: The Science Behind Why Hugs Are So Great

Let's talk about one of the simplest, yet most powerful forms of self-care: the hug. Whether it's a warm embrace after a long day or a Saturday snuggle session with the kids, there's something undeniably comforting about being wrapped up in the arms of someone you love. But did you know there's actual science behind why hugs feel so good? That's right—those warm fuzzies are backed by biology!

When you hug someone (or have a family cuddle pile during movie night), your body releases a cocktail of feel-good hormones. First up is oxytocin, also known as the "love hormone," which helps you feel bonded to the people around you. Then there's serotonin, which boosts your mood and reduces stress, and endorphins, which act as natural painkillers and stress relievers. It's like a free dose of happiness, no prescription required.

Aside from making you feel all warm and fuzzy inside, regular cuddling actually has long-term health benefits. It can lower blood pressure, reduce anxiety, and even improve your immune system. So really, those lazy Saturday morning snuggles are basically medicinal. Who knew that prioritizing some couch cuddles could be as good for you as a green smoothie (and a lot more fun)?

In the hustle of daily life, it's easy to skip the snuggles in favor of checking off another to-do. But making time for those hugs, especially with your kids, is like refilling your emotional tank. It's a reminder that in the midst of all the chaos, the most important thing is the connection you share with the people you love.

So, embrace the power of cuddles. Whether it's a Saturday morning snuggle-fest or a cozy movie night where everyone's piled on the couch, don't underestimate the magic of a good hug. After all, you're not just boosting their happiness—you're boosting yours, too.

CONCLUSION

Parenting Isn't One-Size-Fits-All

Parenting is often treated like a puzzle with one "perfect" solution, but the reality is, there's no single approach that works for everyone. Every family is unique, and each child brings their own blend of personality, quirks, and needs to the table. The best parenting strategy isn't found in any one book, blog, or passing comment from a stranger in the grocery aisle. Instead, it's the approach that feels right for you and your family, even if it means ignoring opinions from the sidelines.

Outsiders will always have their judgments and unsolicited advice, but your parenting journey is yours alone. Trusting your instincts, making room for flexibility, and adapting as your kids grow is what will make you the parent they need. It's less about reaching some "perfect" end and more about committing to growth. Keep learning from what works and what doesn't, and remember, no two families—or even two kids—are exactly alike.

This journey is a lot like the "Plan, Do, Check, Act" cycle. Plan with intention, try it out, reflect on what's working (and what's not), and adjust as you go. Sometimes, you'll nail it on the first try. Other times, you'll need a few iterations. And that's okay! The heart of great parenting isn't about perfect execution—it's about showing up, learning, and loving. So, embrace the highs and the lows, and know that every step brings you closer to the parent your kids need you to be.

www.ingramcontent.com/pod-product-compliance
Lightning Source LLC
Chambersburg PA
CBHW060851050426
42453CB00008B/933